Special Thanks to MATT ABELS

 Alfred Music Publishing Co., Inc.
16320 Roscoe Blvd., Suite 100
P.O. Box 10003
Van Nuys, CA 91410-0003
alfred.com

ISBN-10: 0-7390-4358-7
ISBN-13: 978-0-7390-4358-5

CONTENTS

Producer's Note

On May 8, 1975, *Singin' In The Rain* returned to the big screen at New York's legendary Radio City Music Hall for a special one-week limited run. The film had originally opened there on March 27, 1952, and went on to break the theater's box-office record during its initial engagement. This success was indicative of the response that met the film in theaters all around the world.

In the ensuing years *Singin' In The Rain*'s reputation among film critics, scholars, and fans only heightened. By the time screenwriters Betty Comden and Adolph Green crafted their introduction to the publication of its screenplay in 1972, *Singin' In The Rain* was already a legend, considered by many to be the greatest movie musical ever made.

In 1974 the unexpected box-office sensation caused by M-G-M's *That's Entertainment!* brought renewed attention to the studio's incomparable musicals, especially *Singin' In The Rain*. This inspired M-G-M to give *Singin'* a new chance at theatrical success with the special week-long engagement at Radio City Music Hall.

But no one at the studio or the venerable movie palace expected the half-page laudatory *New York Times* piece that their then-film critic Vincent Canby had written, which appeared in anticipation of the film's upcoming return to Radio City. Canby's article was a brilliantly crafted and unprecedented love letter to the film; he stated that it was "An extraordinarily exuberant, always youthful, joyously indestructible musical." He continued to say that "Enjoying *Singin' In The Rain* has nothing to do with nostalgia or sentimentality. It is simply stated . . . a Hollywood masterpiece." Canby's article took M-G-M, Radio City, and New York itself by surprise. The film went on to do outstanding business during that one week, grossing nearly $200,000. Once again lines wrapped around 49th Street past 5th Avenue to St. Patrick's Cathedral, as thousands of New Yorkers waited to see Kelly & Co. on the music hall's enormous screen. The fact that the film cast its magic over that audience in 1975 in the same way it did when it originally opened undoubtedly proved Canby was right. The film was, and remains, thoroughly "indestructible." Filled with timeless wit and peerless musical entertainment, *Singin' In The Rain* only gets better with age. It continues to beguile new audiences, who are enraptured by its countless pleasures. Through the advent of home video, its popularity has become even more astounding, ultimately surpassing that of all other M-G-M musicals. Although more than a quarter century has passed since that return engagement, Mr. Canby's words about *Singin' In The Rain* are as meaningful as ever. They honor an amazing cinematic achievement by an unprecedented group of great talents who indeed created "a Hollywood masterpiece."

To commemorate *Singin' In The Rain*'s "golden anniversary," Turner Classic Movies Music/Rhino Movie Music takes great pride in presenting this special deluxe edition of the film's soundtrack. Not only do we present the film's score in its entirety, along with alternate and unused takes, but we also present the original versions of these songs, as they first appeared in the M-G-M films of 1929-39, which brought them to public fame. Many of these older recordings are being released here for the first time in their original form. In addition, we present some special archival bonus tracks. All selections have been remastered from the original prerecording session masters (where available).

—George Feltenstein

THE STORY BEHIND
SINGIN' IN THE RAIN:
NOW IT CAN BE TOLD

A NOTE FROM THE AUTHORS:

We wrote the following essay as a preface to the 1972 publication of our *Singin' In The Rain* screenplay. It shares our extraordinary experiences working in the Freed Unit during production of the film, so we felt it would be a fitting addition to this exciting soundtrack album.

All we knew about our assignment when we arrived in Hollywood in late May 1950 was that we were to write an original story and screenplay, as well as the lyrics, for a new musical picture. We had rushed out there in answer to an urgent "there's-not-a-moment-to-lose" crisis command from M-G-M, only to find every studio shut down and the whole place deserted. It looked very much the way Hollywood does right now on an average business day. Actually, all that had happened then was that everyone had taken off for a six-day Decoration Day weekend, leaving us to grind our teeth to the eyeballs in frustration, and run up six days of epic phone bills calling our loved ones back East.

At the time we were pioneers in bicoastal living, continuing to write for the theater in New York, our home, and coming out West periodically, to do a movie, and then return. By then we had written several pictures, the latest of which was the adaptation of our first Broadway show, *On The Town*. The film had enjoyed financial and critical success, and the public happily accepted the concept of an intimate movie musical in which almost all the musical numbers were handled by a small group of principals in realistic situations, some of them actually photographed on location in the streets of New York. It was also the first directorial assignment for Gene Kelly and Stanley Donen.

We always worked in what was known as the "Freed Unit." This was presided over by producer Arthur Freed from his three-room office suite in the imposing Thalberg or Administration Building, affectionately called "the Iron Lung." Our office was a simple monastic cell down the hall, which, because of our transiency, we never tried to make even remotely livable. The Freed Unit was something quite special in Hollywood, with

BY BETTY COMDEN AND ADOLPH GREEN

conditions that permitted us to function somewhat the way we would in doing a show in New York. The writer was not treated as part of an assembly line in the old Hollywood tradition, which placed him at the bottom of the social structure, with the ego-crushing certainty that forty other scriptwriters would obliterate any trace of his work before it reached the screen. (Writers were considered "the authors" unless disastrously proved otherwise, and were usually included in discussion of all aspects of production.) Arthur also had a gift for importing, or taking chances on, people of the theater, allowing them to develop into moviemakers with a free-swinging spirit—Vincente Minnelli, Gene Kelly, Stanley Donen, Alan Jay Lerner, Oliver Smith, Michael Kidd, and the two of us. Down through the years and up until today, Arthur Freed has always referred to us as "the kids," sometimes warmly, as in "Hiya, kids" or "I'd like you to meet 'the

kids,'" or sometimes impatiently (at a story conference), as in "For Chrissakes, kids, no one will believe that!" Assisting in all departments, as musical supervisor, sometimes script shepherd, arranger, associate producer, general coordinator of production—sometimes one or all of these—was Roger Edens, invaluable and devoted to Freed, and whose lapels we often clutched, and drenched with tears in moments of despair. In the late forties and early fifties the musicals emerging from this group, conducted and orchestrated mainly by Lennie Hayton and Conrad Salinger, had a kind of style and taste, filmic verve and inventiveness, that gave them the individual stamp of the Freed Unit, and a number of them survive, not as "camp" or sociological curiosa, but as films to be enjoyed, admired, and even wondered at—expressions of a form that has all but vanished.

When everyone returned from their interminable holiday that June in 1950, we were summoned, unslept and nervous, to a meeting in Arthur's office, where we were finally to discover why we had been rushed out there. Sun-drenched and relaxed after his rest, and surrounded by orchids from his vast greenhouses, Arthur greeted us warmly, inquired after families and friends, quoted the grosses of South Pacific from *Variety*, and read us letters from Giancarlo Menotti and Irving Berlin, and after some further discussion of the state of the theater in New York, and phone calls to his brother Hugo at the orchid ranch, and to Oscar Levant on Stage 27, he said, "C'mon, kids, let's have some lunch." Arthur was trying not to tell us something.

Somewhere around four that afternoon, after some prodding from us, he let it be known with a proud but shy chuckle that we had been assigned to write an original story and screenplay using songs from the extensive catalogue of lyricist Arthur Freed (the same) and composer Nacio Herb Brown (how many people can there be named "Nacio Herb Brown"?). Whatever came out of our creative hoppers, or out of two hopping mad creators, was to be called *Singin' In The Rain*. We gulped a gulp that could be heard around the world, and then followed a long silence during which the orchids around us seemed to grow into the man-eating variety. Finally we said, "But, Arthur, what about our new contract? It says, with all names spelled out, that Comden and Green are to write the lyrics unless the score is by (1) Irving Berlin, (2) Cole Porter, (3) Rodgers and Hammerstein." Arthur said, "Kids, I never heard of any such clause. Now, about *Singin' In The Rain*—" Bolstered by our knowledge of that magical clause, we sneered imperiously, skulked out of the office, and went on strike. After two war-torn weeks, during which we repeatedly accused Arthur of reneging on an official document, some flutter of the gut told us to read our contract. With the help of our new agent, Irving Lazar, using his bifocals as the Geiger counter to unearth the magical phrase, we learned there was no such thing. It was the emperor's new clause, a total fabrication of our former agent. "Kids," said Irving, "anyone can write lyrics for your picture—Berlin, Porter, R. and H., Freed, Karloff, Lugosi, Johnny Weissmuller—you name it. My suggestion is you write 'Singin' In The Rain' at the top of a page, followed by 'Fade-in,' and don't stop until you come to 'That's all, folks.'" So we began working on *Singin' In The Rain* like rats trapped in a burning barn. And let it be known for the record that Freed was very sweet and tolerant with us rats— didn't chase us with a broom or anything.

Later that very day we met with Roger around his piano in the Freed office and surveyed the sprawling stacks of Freed-Brown songs in sheet-music form, ranging all the way from "Should I?" to "Would You?" The late sun was just hitting the sign outside Smith and Salisbury, Mortuary next door, and we felt like walking over and lying down. We riffled through the songs as Roger played and sang them in his Southern colonel's whiskey baritone, and several possible stories suggested themselves. For instance, "The Wedding Of The Painted Doll" could well have been the basis for a story about a painted doll who got married.

But as Roger kept playing, we hummed along, we began in spite of ourselves to get excited. Many of them were famous songs, standards, bristling with vitality and part of the nation's collective unconscious—"Broadway Melody," "Broadway Rhythm," "You Are My Lucky Star," "Fit As A Fiddle," "You Were Meant For Me," and the title song itself, an irresistible ode to optimism which no one can possibly sing without acting out the line "There's a smile on my face."

We knew one thing about the story. There would have to be some scene where there would be rain, and the leading man (Howard Keel? Van Johnson? Fred Astaire? Gene Kelly?) would be singin' in it. Many of these songs had been written by Freed and Brown for the earliest musical pictures made, between 1929 and 1931, during the painful transition from silent to sound, and it occurred to us that, rather than try to use them in a sophisticated, contemporary story, or a gay-nineties extravaganza, they would bloom at their happiest in something that took place in the very period in which they had been written. With this decision made we began to feel the ground beneath our feet at last. We both knew the period intimately and were amateur authorities on silent films and early talkies, long before Cinema 1 and 2 was a subject taught in every kindergarten in the country.

The studio grapevine reached us that Howard Keel had been penciled in for the lead, and we made a few dispirited stabs at a yarn about a minor Western actor in silents who makes it big with the advent of sound as a singing cowboy.

But our thoughts kept coming back to the dramatic upheavals of that period, when great careers were wrecked because the public's image of a favorite would be instantly destroyed by a voice that did not match the fabled face. We remembered particularly the downfall of John Gilbert, the reigning king of the silent screen in 1928, whose career was finished off by one talking picture, in which, with his director's encouragement, he improvised his own love scene, consisting of the phrase "I love you" repeated many times with growing intensity, exactly as he had done it the year before in front of the silent camera. The audience screamed with laughter. We decided our leading character should be just such a star. The trick, of course, was to make the stuff of tragedy like this fit into a lighthearted satirical comedy that featured fifteen or twenty Freed-Brown songs along the way. Our silent star would have to survive his downfall and make good as a musical star, and to give that story point a faint air of credibility, we had better establish our hero as someone who had had a song-and-dance vaudeville background before he entered pictures. Such a character felt more to us like Gene Kelly than Howard Keel. Gene was one of our oldest friends

7

from New York, as was Stanley Donen. We had first met Gene when we were in a revue at the Westport Country Playhouse one summer, he hoofing it up alone, and the two of us performing as part of a satirical act called "The Revuers." Later, when we had reached the dizzy heights of the Rainbow Room, Gene, still an unknown, was suddenly announced by the M.C. there as doing a tryout appearance for one show. Not long after, our paths crossed again, when he, the newly acclaimed Broadway star of *Pal Joey*, came down to the Village Vanguard to see his old pals, The Revuers, who had followed their heady climb to the sixty-fifth floor of the RCA Building by plummeting swiftly back down to the Vanguard cellar where they had started. Later, in Hollywood, a big movie star, Gene was to feed us often, and watch us perform tirelessly in his living room, writing having replaced performing in our careers, but not in our hearts and throats. Stanley was there, too, having started as a dancer in *Pal Joey*, and coming out to Hollywood when Gene did, to work as his assistant, and then co-director.

After their outstanding success as the directing team of *On The Town*, what we none too secretly hoped for was to reunite the four of us, with Gene again as star. But Gene was now, deservedly, at that happy moment when everyone wanted him for everything, and had he expressed the desire to film Kafka's *Metamorphosis* featuring the "Million-Legged Cockroach Ballet," the studio would have considered it a smart commercial move, and gone all the way with him. It was impossible for us to approach him, because he was deeply involved, head and feet, starring in and choreographing *An American In Paris*, which was shooting on the lot under Vincente Minnelli's direction. We kept seeing him all the time socially, but he let us know, in a friendly way, he was going to pick his next venture very carefully, and would rather not know what we were up to, so he could judge the finished script impartially.

In the meantime we spent an agonizing month trying to get a grip on ourselves and our screenplay. We finally had what seemed to be three possible opening sequences of a picture: a big silent-movie premiere in New York; a magazine interview with the star in Hollywood telling a phony life story; a sequence from the silent movie being premiered in New York, the star meeting the girl in New York, losing her, and going back to Hollywood. After staring for hours at a time at this seemingly insoluble mess, in which the story never seemed to get started, we would wander down to the set where *An American In Paris* was shooting, and feel even more wretched in the face of this assured, inevitably successful reality, rolling along with its thundering playbacks, swinging cranes, and jubilant actors, and its little Paris street, so achingly authentic that Arthur Freed could sit in the sidewalk café and quip to no one in particular, "I can sit here and feel homesick for Hollywood."

Our depression deepened as our story refused to move, and our feeling that we were involved in something ghoulish rather than comic was reinforced by the atmosphere of the place we were living in. It was a miniature Sunset Boulevard house, once owned by silent star Marie Prevost, which we had taken with mixed laughter and shudders because the price was right. The place screamed, in its tattered elegance, of high times in the twenties, with its glory suddenly extinguished. There was no body floating in the swimming pool, but tons of soggy leaves filled the deeper-than-wide concrete oblong, gloomily hidden from the sun at all times of the day; torn strips of faded awning flapped mournfully against the terrace windows; and inside the living room, furnished mainly with peeling gilt and needlepoint pieces and an urn containing God knows whose ashes, was the crowning touch—an inlaid concert grand player piano, its piano roll stuck from there to eternity somewhere in the middle of "Fascinatin' Rhythm." It was in this very room, one late afternoon, that we decided to kick the nightmarish grip of doom that had settled over us, and do something realistic: we would give M-G-M back the money they had paid us thus far, tell them we had failed, and go home.

A couple of hours later we were jumping up and down with glee, like Gene, Donald, and Debbie in the "Good Morning" song and dance in the movie *Singin' In The Rain* itself. My (Betty's) husband, Steve, had just arrived from New York and, knowing us rather well, was not too surprised to find us slumped in our familiar Dostoyevskian attitudes. At some point we grabbed him and read him our goulash of openings, to illustrate the hopelessness of the situation. Much to our amazement, Steve, a reticent chuckler, was roaring throughout, and asked, offhandedly, why, instead of abandoning the project, didn't we use all the openings? This led to the Eureka moment of realizing that maybe it could work if the action never went to New York, but all took place in Hollywood: the premiere, the interview in front of the theater before the stars go in, the shots of the silent movie itself, the backstage scene, the star's escape from his fans and his meeting the girl on Hollywood Boulevard, instead of Fifth Avenue. It seems pitifully obvious now, bordering on the moronic, but at the time we felt like Champollion deciphering the Rosetta Stone. From here on, the gates were open and the writing of the screenplay gushed in a relatively exuberant flow. We tapped the roots of our memories and experiences without editing ourselves when our ideas got wild,

satirical, and extravagantly nonsensical. To our gratified surprise, not only did Roger seem delighted with it all, but Arthur, to whom we read each section as we completed it, gave it his happy approval. (The final go-ahead had to come from Dore Schary, who had recently replaced L. B. Mayer as head of the studio.)

At Arthur's suggestion, Gene, who was by now finished shooting *An American In Paris*, was given a script to read, and we geared ourselves for a friendly refusal. Instead, he and Stanley Donen, who had also read it, came rushing over to us in the commissary the next day bursting with enthusiasm and filled with ideas which they imparted to us over our usual lunch of L. B. Mayer matzo-ball soup and surrealist song parodies. We started meeting with them instantly for final changes and rewrites, going over the script shot by shot. In addition to their outstanding skill in integrating all the elements of a musical film, our old friendship with them, and their knowledge of our work from our early performing days, made it easy for them to use many ideas and visual details that might have seemed irrelevant or a total mystery to anyone else.

The success of the film and its continued life over the years has much to do with our four-way mental radar, Gene and Stanley's brilliant execution, and their sure professionalism while maintaining an air of effortless, carefree spontaneity. Also, one of the two directors gave a great performance. Just as we knew from the start, there was a scene where there was rain, and the leading man was singin' in it.

What we hadn't written into the script was "Here Gene Kelly does perhaps the outstanding solo number of his career." Today, ironically enough, this exuberant, joyous expression of love of life is achieving a new kind of identity through Stanley Kubrick's *A Clockwork Orange*, where it is so devastatingly and chillingly used as an a cappella song and dance of mindless violence.

We went back to New York, leaving behind a lyric composed of tongue twisters starting with "Moses supposes his toes-es are roses," which Roger Edens put to music, making it the one non-Freed-Brown contribution to the score. We also learned, as the shooting day approached, that "The Wedding Of The Painted Doll," which we had painfully wedged into the script as a cheering-up number for Donald O'Connor, had been replaced by a new song by Arthur and Mr. Brown, "Make 'Em Laugh." For this number Gene and Stanley took every piece of zany gymnastic clowning and surrealist vaudeville bit Donald had saved up in his body, and worked them into an insane classic unlike any other before or since.

Some months later, while out-of-town in Philadelphia going through the life-and-death throes of a revue we were involved with, we got a call from Gene and Stanley which seemed by that time to be coming from another galaxy.

We had written a protracted love scene with a song-and-dance medley for Gene and Debbie Reynolds that involved touring many different sets all over the studio lot, but our directors wanted to change all that to a romantic lover scene inside an empty sound stage where Gene would sing one song only, and do a romantic dance with Debbie. Could we run it up and mail it right out, please? We wrenched our minds away from the great Bert Lahr just two blocks away at the Shubert Theatre despondently being hilarious in the ninety-five degree July Philadelphia heat, and time-machined ourselves back into *Singin' In The Rain* long enough to fill the order. It worked. So did the picture.

A few years ago we were in Paris with my (Betty's) husband, Steve, and my (Adolph's) wife, Phyllis, at a party, and were rendered breathless and awe-struck by the news that François Truffaut was right across the room from us. Suddenly a small, lithe figure came sliding across at us like a hockey player zooming over the ice. It was Truffaut himself, and he was breathless and awe-struck at meeting the authors of Chantons sous la pluie. In total disbelief we heard him go on to say, through his interpreter, that he had seen the film many many times, knew every frame of

14

it, felt it was a classic, and that he and Alain Resnais, among others, went to see it regularly at a little theater called the Pagode, where it was even at that moment in the middle of a several-month run. This is a scene we never could have dreamed of that day at M-G-M when we went on strike because we did not want to write anything to be called *Singin' In The Rain*.

Nor could we have known that *Time* magazine would refer to it as one of the great "watershed" pictures (we have been assured it's not because of the title), or that Pauline Kael would one day write of it, "This exuberant and malicious satire of Hollywood in the late twenties is perhaps the most enjoyable of all movie musicals—just about the best Hollywood musical of all time."

Betty Comden and Adolph Green

From *Singin' In The Rain*, "Introduction," by Betty Comden and Adolph Green, Copyright © 1972 by The Viking Press, Inc. Used by permission of Viking Penguin, a division of Penguin Books U.S.A. Inc.

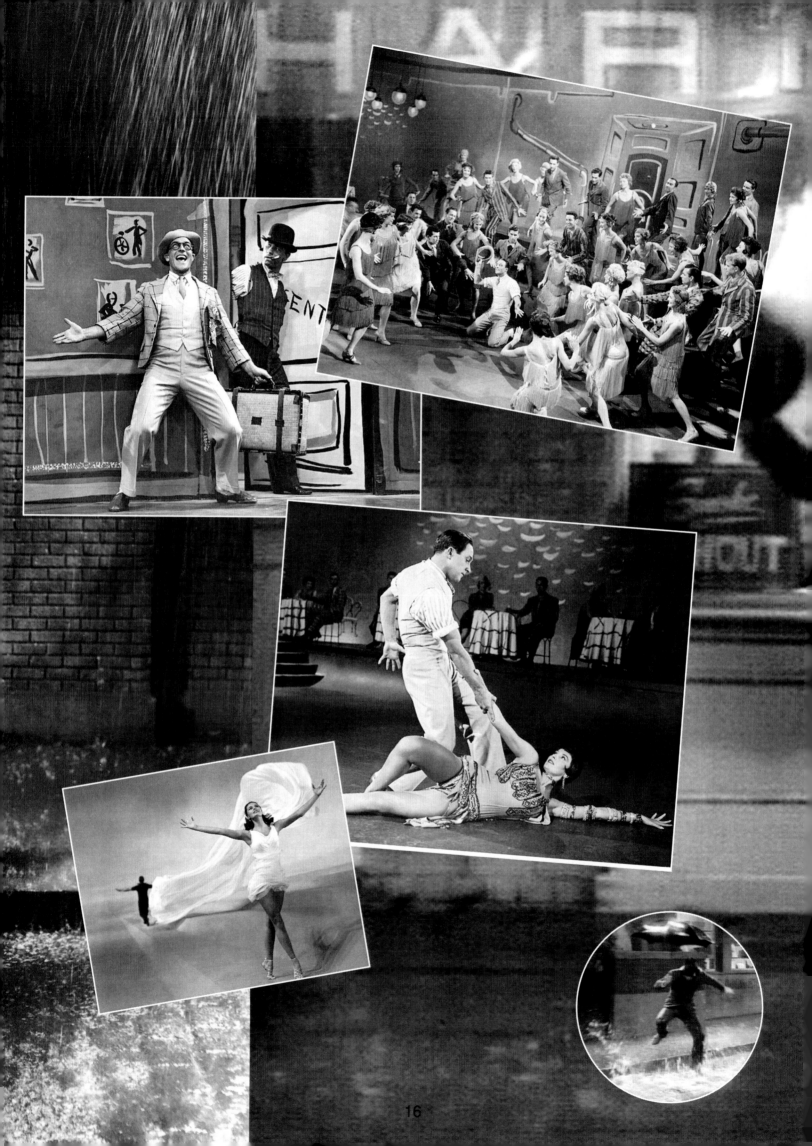

GOOD MORNING

Lyric by
ARTHUR FREED

Music by
NACIO HERB BROWN

Good Morning - 3 - 1
26121

ALL I DO IS DREAM OF YOU

Lyric by
ARTHUR FREED

Music by
NACIO HERB BROWN

BROADWAY MELODY

Lyric by
ARTHUR FREED

Music by
NACIO HERB BROWN

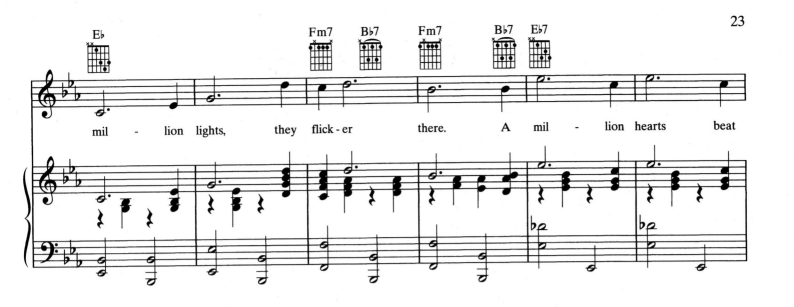

mil - lion lights, they flick - er there. A mil - lion hearts beat

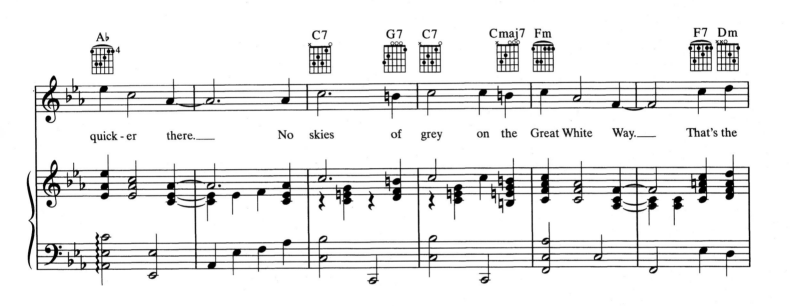

quick - er there.___ No skies of grey on the Great White Way.___ That's the

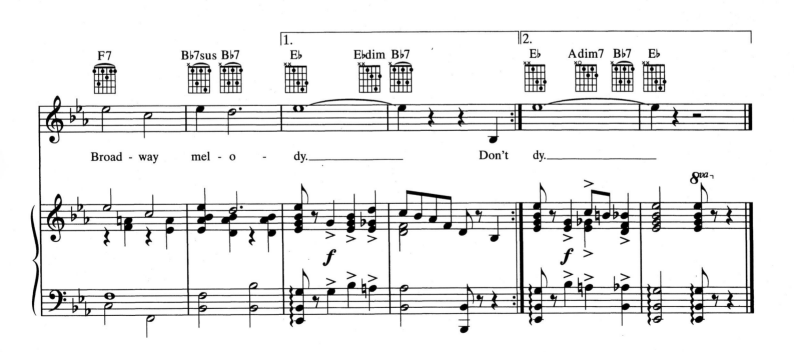

Broad - way mel - o - dy._____ Don't dy._____

BROADWAY RHYTHM

Lyric by
ARTHUR FREED

Music by
NACIO HERB BROWN

Got - ta dance! Got - ta dance!

Got - ta dance! Got - ta dance!

Broad - way rhy - thm, it's got me. Ev - 'ry - bod - y

Broadway Rhythm - 5 - 1
26121

Fine

Oh, _____ that Broad - way

rhy - thm. _____

Oh, _____ that Broad - way

rhy - thm. _____

D.S. % al Fine

FIT AS A FIDDLE

Lyric by
ARTHUR FREED

Music by
AL HOFFMAN
and AL GOODHEART

I'VE GOT A FEELIN' YOU'RE FOOLIN'

Lyric by
ARTHUR FREED

Music by
NACIO HERB BROWN

MAKE 'EM LAUGH

Lyric by
ARTHUR FREED

Music by
NACIO HERB BROWN

Make 'em laugh,_____ make 'em
roar,_____ make 'em

laugh._____ Don't you know ev - 'ry - one wants to
scream._____ Don't you know all the world wants to

laugh?_____ My dad said, "Be an
laugh?_____ My grand - pa said, "Go out and

Make 'Em Laugh - 3 - 1
26121

MOSES

Words by
BETTY COMDEN
and ADOLPH GREEN

Music by
ROGER EDENS

SHOULD I

Lyric by
ARTHUR FREED

Music by
NACIO HERB BROWN

SINGIN' IN THE RAIN

Lyric by
ARTHUR FREED

Music by
NACIO HERB BROWN

To Coda ⊕

lane with a hap - py re - frain, and sing - in',___ just sing - in' in___ the

G6   E♭7

rain._____

Why   am   I   smil - in',   and
Why   do they call   me   the

G6   E♭7

why   do   I   sing?___   Why   does De - cem - ber   seem
boy with the smile?___   When   did   I   find   out   that

G6   D7

sun - ny   as   spring?___   Why   do   I   get   up   each
life is   worth - while?___   Why   do   I   treat   all   my

TEMPTATION

Lyric by
ARTHUR FREED

Music by
NACIO HERB BROWN

Moderately, with feeling

WOULD YOU?

Lyric by
ARTHUR FREED

Music by
NACIO HERB BROWN

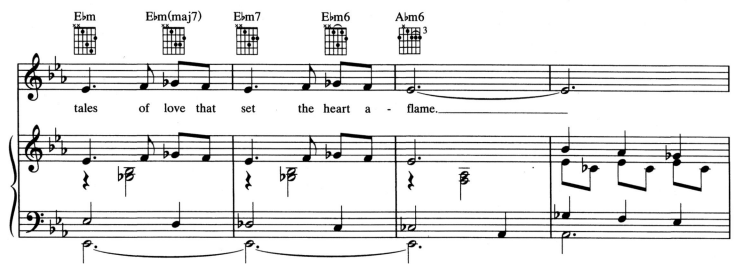

I've been read-ing such ro-man-tic sto-ries,

tales of love that set the heart a - flame.

THE WEDDING OF THE PAINTED DOLL

Lyric by
ARTHUR FREED

Music by
NACIO HERB BROWN

YOU ARE MY LUCKY STAR

Lyric by
ARTHUR FREED

Music by
NACIO HERB BROWN

YOU WERE MEANT FOR ME

Lyric by
ARTHUR FREED

Music by
NACIO HERB BROWN